Voluntary Servitude

BOOKS BY MARK WUNDERLICH

The Anchorage
Voluntary Servitude
The Earth Avails

Voluntary Servitude

POEMS BY

Mark Wunderlich

Graywolf Press

Publication of this volume is made possible in part by a grant provided by the Minnesota State Arts Board, through an appropriation by the Minnesota State Legislature; a grant from the Wells Fargo Foundation Minnesota; and a grant from the National Endowment for the Arts, which believes that a great nation deserves great art. Significant support has also been provided by the Bush Foundation; Target, Marshall Field's and Mervyn's with support from the Target Foundation; the McKnight Foundation; and other generous contributions from foundations, corporations, and individuals. To these organizations and individuals we offer our heartfelt thanks.

Special funding for this title has been provided by the Jerome Foundation.

MINNESOTA
STATE ARTS BOARD

NATIONAL
ENDOWMENT
FOR THE ARTS

Published by Graywolf Press
250 Third Avenue North, Suite 600
Minneapolis, Minnesota 55401
All rights reserved.

www.graywolfpress.org

Published in the United States of America

ISBN 978-1-55597-408-4

2 4 6 8 9 7 5 3

Library of Congress Control Number: 2004104188

Cover design: Kyle G. Hunter

Cover photo: doublepoint/Photonica

Table of Contents

For James Cancienne —

Me dire une histoire.

. . . and let the pleasure we invent together
be one more sign of freedom.

—Julio Cortázar

Voluntary Servitude

Amaryllis

after Rilke

You've seen a cat consume a hummingbird,
scoop its beating body from the pyracantha bush
and break its wings with tufted paws
before marshaling it, whole, into its bone-tough throat;
seen a boy, heart racing with cocaine, climb
from a car window to tumble on the ground,
his search for pleasure ending in skinned palms;
heard a woman's shouts as she is pushed into the police cruiser,
large hand pressing her head into the door,
red lights spinning their tornado in the street.

But all of that will fade; on the table is the amaryllis
pushing its monstrous body in the air,
requiring no soil to do so, having wound
two seasons' rot into a white and papered bulb,
exacting nutrition from the winter light,
culling from complex chemistry the tints
and fragments that tissue and pause and build
again the pigment and filament.
The flower crescendos toward the light,
though better to say despite it,
gores through gorse and pebble
to form a throat—so breakable—open
with its tender pistils, damp with rosin,
simple in its simple sex, to burn and siphon
itself in air. Tongue of fire, tongue
of earth, the amaryllis is a rudiment
forming its meretricious petals
to trumpet and exclaim.

How you admire it. It vibrates
in the draft, a complex wheel
bitten with cogs, swelling and sexual
though nothing will touch it. You forced it
to spread itself, to cleave and grasp,
remorseless, open to your assignments—
this is availability, this is tenderness,
this red plane is given to the world.
Sometimes the heart breaks. Sometimes
it is not held hostage. The red world
where cells prepare for the unexpected
splays open at the window's ledge.
Be not human you inhuman thing.
No anxious, no foible, no hesitating hand.
Pry with fiber your course through sand.
Point your whole body toward the unknown
away from the dead.
Be water and light and land—
no contrivance, no gasp, no dream
where there is no head.

Voluntary Servitude

In a valley in Wisconsin there is a graveyard where the graves are flooded by a spring.

You say, Don't wreck me, and I say I won't, but how can I know that?

To see a man in shackles, how you feel about that, depends on whether the
   servitude is voluntary.

The bodies are intact in their graves, soaked in a bath of ice. Hair a net around them.

Music does not console me. Words in books rise up and scatter.

A friend told me of a snake that came into her room one night.

The house was in Pennsylvania. She lived there alone.

In the dark she could hear it—dry, slipping onto boards like a stocking rolled
   from a leg.

It retreated when she turned on a light. There was a dark hole at the floor.

Residents disagree about the cemetery.

Some think to say the bodies are intact is wrong.

To suggest that there is anything abnormal is unfit thinking.

I have a new story to tell you.

In it, there is a girl. It's a story a friend once told me.

Some forms of servitude are voluntary. Some shackles too—

Some you can remove. But this story—

you start in the middle, in the thick and marrow of it.

I think you'll like it. Let me tell it to you.

Lying side by side. In the dark.

Lamb

Inside the sheep's hot center, lambs tangle,
soft joints press a tender twin.

I am brought to the barn, soap my arm in a sink.
Orion stabs the sky with his arrow of ice.

I unwrap one sister from her awakening sister,
carefully, for the flesh is tender and this is an animal will.

Hand in the cave where blood shapes into an other,
I will bring them forth, bleating into January.

Good shepherd, I will shelter them from fangs,
chase stray dogs with a gun, turn them onto grass in spring.

They will come when I call, press against woven wire
even though I call them to the gleaming hook.

Tack

Bridle and martingale,
the crupper's strap and buckle,

hobble and tassel binds
the mare to matter. Crack

of the crop's split flap on a flank.
Push begged the animal,

Push begged the man
and the two sprang out,

half-moon of mud flung
from a hoof. Finger flick,

check bit, metal on the tongue
leather in the hand,

knee turn to saddle girdle,
girth gives a little, looser.

Speed is the animal
wish is the man—

curve the neck, roll the eye
the jump is high

but will is all. Pull
strap, fit thigh,

skin covers muscle,
matter is the mind.

Letter to J.

With your hand over my mouth, your body on my back, I still attempt refusal. In my head, the tattered curtain falls to the stage, the actors give over iron-scorched costumes to the laundress, the carts are wheeled away with their props of paste.

Your mother interests me. Today I think of her lying in the cool recess of your plantation home, splayed in her negligee upon the candlewick spread, her six French boys on their knees around her, a rosary clicking off sins bead by bead.

Once you told me of the house maid who spilled her change on the front porch—money she'd pinched from your pockets in the laundry. You knelt to help her gather it up. The money didn't matter to you, though her small revenge clings to you like a burr.

I pretend you are the father. I am the child stepping into the bath. My pale limbs texture with gooseflesh and the water is too hot. When I call, you come to me, wash my small body, which once was your body and curled in the smallest cell of your sex. You handle me gently but with contempt.

Your teeth have left their impress on my thigh. When you hurt me, I press my face to the pillow and do my sums. Two wings and a feathery heart do not add up to bird. Fathers and sons continue to multiply.

Landscape Dream #7

As a child I was taken in a boat

onto the river   Insects buzzed

Small fish rose to the surface

and receded

The boat's motor when it cut out

made the other sounds large

We drifted toward an island

separated from the banks by a channel

drifted in the shade provided

by a canopy of trees

But soon we noticed them

cutting their S's in the brown water

slipping their dry lengths

over green branches   Black

and airless they took things from us

took the small breaths

from our tightening chests

Their eyes held no light

Absorbed nothing

But it was more than that

The snakes hanging from the canopy

dropping

into the water around us

twisting like the ink across a text

divided the world in half

Breakable

Water and sand and everything shining. Dogs bursting in and out of the scene. Even the dull mats of seaweed glitter, cold morning. I appreciate all of this from my window with its superior view.

You're still sleeping in a city three thousand miles away. Arms, wrists, bare feet lax, bedclothes twisted about you. I know those beginnings with their fog and distant sirens, worktable and food to prepare, walking softly to let you lie.

In Bavaria there was a madwoman who thought she'd swallowed a glass piano, its ungodly crystal pinging away as she moved. Servants carried her on her cushioned palanquin and she cried out from the slightest touch. Burdened by her treasure, rare, her nerves scared up like a devil, she grew thin, but the instrument held its shape within her.

It is winter here in this unreal town. A painter is putting graphite to prepared canvas, illustrating a fairy-tale breast pricked by a thorn. A rose grows there, larks drink and bleed vines of blood, a woman rides her diminutive horse, false mother's severed head weeping in her lap. The woman wears a mask of a dog, tongue lolling. There is so much in the world that is breaking, so many acts of revenge.

Bed of feathers, sand tracked in, I sweep and sweep. If there's an other with you now, don't tell me. I want my bright morning untouched by an other's tongue.

Dream of Archeology

On the desert hardpan, we set our brushes twitching
to uncover the chips scattered across what had once been a temple.

Nine gates opened in the wind, nine gates no longer visible.
Soon, I found the broken tibia, the net of bones

I recognized as human and my own brush dusted away
the crumbled attar of the grave.

Dust rose up. A shape announced itself to me. Inside
the cracked bowl of a pelvis my mind sketched in a face.

A thing was carried there that met the world with its wet and blood-tender
head. The sun sent down its burning sentence, even and ill-willed

as we disturbed the sleeping mother I begged would forgive
this intrusion. Though my question would be answered with decay.

Device for Burning Bees and Sugar

It marks a grave.

Touch the sugar to your lips, ensuring its consistency, the amber pearl.

In the pan of hammered copper.

Collect the bees keeping in mind that on chill days or in fog, the hive remains sluggish. Wild bees offer distinct features, favoring thistle and columbine. Domestic bees are more still with essence of apple and clover bloom.

Release them from their trap into a bell jar. Fifty or sixty bees should suffice.

(Last night, the spring dream—finches beating the bars at the window, light mist.)

In the clearing, build a fire of dogwood and dung. A slow flame is required.

Prepare your text. Before you, many have come. Accordingly, the site you choose may well be a grave. Bodies pushed into the soil; bodies pushing up through the soil. Your text will be the needle point of remembrance. Belt this to your waist with the kidskin harness.

On the appointed morning bathe in water floated with white carnations.

Do this to satisfy the ghost.

Off and off and off.

As you read your text, the shadows will swell.

Release the bees one by one, feeding them into the device. As they touch the surface of the pan, the smoke will become a garment around you. In your hive of smoke, a calm will settle.

Inside you, a field will open outward.

The dead and their whispers cannot find you there

in a world of burning light and pollen.

Dream: Intruder

A storm boiled the ocean.
The room's heavy timbers shifted
as the wind pushed the town.

Beside you, I dreamed I saw a ghost.
Blond and ageless, he mocked me
with large teeth, slipped his arm

around your tan shoulder
and cradled your neck
with what once was his hand.

I cursed him
for stepping through the membrane
of his world into mine,

for pressing to you
his T-shirt and faded jeans
which he must have worn in life

and were now a bitter shroud.
Like a ship's hold, the room swayed
as I fixed him with narrowed eyes

and pointed with one finger,
forbidding him to ever come again.
You remained sleeping

unaware that he had found us
or that the draft that tarnished the room
blew from the other side.

I Too Am an Animal of Great Beauty

Out of the box came the implements—black cowhide whipstitched into a garment, pants that bind, chest harness and vest, rubber strap. I smelled the salty taint of men who once fit inside you—all of it cinched in the shopping bag of ropes with their maritime stains.

On me or in me, I am learning to hollow, to fashion a room in flesh's house. Hog-tied and hemstitched, gag in my mouth, I want your damage, your tight strung racket batting me back. I am your wrong, your one, your scrapped minuet, the fleur-de-lis tattooed on your ass. Fluids keep us apart. Always the world with its empty syringe.

In our home with its taxidermy and closets of boiled wool, the twin oil portraits stare prissily from early last century. A neighbor listens in while you thump me like a beast. *You're a little pig*, you say sweetly. *You're my little pussy-boy pig.*

And I am like an animal. I walk from front door to back, the light harming me. The pill I've swallowed pulls a white curtain around the metal bed of my brain. You pedal away and I watch from the window. Another lost sailor throws his hat to the bay.

White

Among the birches
ears scooped the rustle.

Ruby, his eyes
increased the rounded world.

No pigment save the sepia stain
the gland between his antlers left.

On sugar legs, he'd melt in winter,
leaving prints, aboriginal,

all animal.
Two lights appeared.

Machinery fit itself
to his blue-toned form.

This paper sheet
mimics him,

snow troubling the picture
as any whiteness will.

Error

He stands on the corner waiting for the light.

(City traffic conducts its next round of business.)

The word I keep coming to is *error.*

Some days, the simplest things grow large and amazing.

All I ever wanted was—

It is hard to avoid sentimentality when speaking of the end.

It is hard to carry thoughts over, moving from day to day.

Exhalation breathes the lovers back into the world.

The *you* here will go on managing the dailiness.

The telephone will be answered, the room crossed—

The *I* will become static, a narrow slash on white.

The *I* will find a certain comfort.

On the corner, a man stands, waiting for the light.

Though now I see the light is green, and something keeps him.

He hesitates.

The *I* assigns certain feelings to the man on the corner.

I will call it a gesture.

In his hesitation, opportunity,

a place where anything might happen.

Water Snake

My grandmother fed it bits of ground meat,

taught it to come when she clapped her hands, or whistled.

The creature spent its days lolling about the boathouse.

Its presence repelled the rats.

The Mississippi lapped its filthy water against corrugated summers

as I jigged my fishing line over the boathouse rail.

The snake looped and glided over the tin roof.

It undulated a thousand tiny muscles to do so.

The sight of it nauseated me—

how it moved like waves of heat rising off a road.

I detest anything that crawls on its belly,

harbors a pallid heart wet with cool blood.

At night, it slid among the bulrushes at the rocky shore

or twisted like a cipher through the black water in search of frogs.

Afternoons, it absorbed the heat of the day

rousing itself only when it heard that familiar whistle

and rose up to receive the gift of flesh

arcing toward it through the air.

Vulpecular Dream #1

Your lower half was a fox—
smell of musk and cold in the underfur,

black-tipped guard hairs
running down the spine. Feral and striving

you muscled through the leaf-rot,
human eyes sharpened to two

red moons. Even across that distance—
your breach from humanity—

I pursued you, knowing full well
I had to be afraid. Your plumed tail twitched,

carnivorous and fine,
paw and hand tracking in the loam,

pricked ear catching
a forest bird's tender radiation,

its small notes broken
on the red plane of your tongue.

The Imperial Life of Insects

There is, in the old city, a museum of living butterflies. The glass walls of the Imperial Greenhouse hold them hostage. Among the tropical rot the insects bloom, bright eyes simulated on powdery tissues. They sip sugars through prehensile tongues, careen in choppy orbs. The heat drove me out. At a cafe table—coffee, chocolate fingers, slate clouds of tobacco smoke—I sketched them badly, their forms terrific and scarce.

I watched your body seize and uncurl. In the morning you told me of your wicked dream—the basket of snakes kept under the dresser, their headless lengths wounded, requiring your attention. In their enclosure they writhe and twine. They are infants. I do not remember my dreams—in the morning, they burn off quickly, hide themselves in pink-lidded shade.

The morning is piano music, cut fruit on a plate. Across the bay, the sun will be more persistent, glance off your upturned face while I try to slow the heart's pattern to something more fragile, thin-winged.

Postcards from the Vienna Woods

From the burning fields, the smoke rose up, whip-thin,
moved toward the city, confirmed by radio reports.

Behind the post office, on the little castle plaza, I saw the covered corridor
where men slept, warmed by their sleeping dogs.

She said, "We have not had an American here since the war,"
and holding the twitching rabbit by the hocks, separated its neck bones.

The mother returned home, scolded her three girls through tears
for using all the butter. "You are selfish girls. I pity your poor husbands."

On the castle plaza, at noon, a drunk pisses in a fountain.
Mothers put their bodies between the spectacle and their children.

"I am not a real German," she insisted. "My mother is from Austria."
The sun crossed from the window and lit her red hair.

A man followed me up the stairs out into the street. The moon
unhooked its tallow figure from the cathedral's green-lit spire.

schweigen *keep or be silent, to say nothing of, not to speak of,*
pass something over in silence, make no reply

I walk slowly so the man can catch up. His steps chafe
the cobblestones in wet air.

I will let him touch me, though we'll never exchange names.
"It is all better to be impersonal, no?" he asks, the grass staining his trousers.

The city absorbs a petty theft, an unsigned letter.
You remain sleeping. I mark steps toward the door.

The Kept One

This is a linden tree. Say it, say *linden.* Tomorrow, you will learn to order breakfast. I will teach you the formula that turns statement into request.

Recently, we experienced a moon more grandiose than any recorded in one hundred and thirty-three years. Bony pastures were whitened. We leaned from third-floor balconies. We brightened while looking into its oracular face.

Birds sing. Other creatures sing, and men sing too. Tonight sound is bound onto tape, but a machine is not a throat, does not know the hurt or tenderness. A machine replays a woman who sang beautifully, who now lies under hardpan in Southern California where she burns. Sometimes a thing dies back but leaves its tone behind.

Once, we lay down in a forest. Rain fell and we were a dry space hollowed out of the rain. Under the night's black timbers, I shivered until you became enough to warm me. Morning broke into heavenly pieces. All was clear. And the ocean? We stopped to see it—seven distances, the day broken up into glass.

Obedience Attempts

The man on my frayed Oriental rug is on all fours. "I'm your little dog, Sir. Treat me like your little brown dog." You'll speak when I tell you to speak, I say. The mind wanders the green hillside in the distance, herds its menagerie toward a better situation.

Afterwards, after spasm and servitude, he pins me to the bed. "I am bigger than you are, Sir. I could hurt you. If I wanted to. But I won't. You're the Sir."

That's right, I say. I'm the Master.

In Vienna, students dash blue paint on the ruins of an Empire. Rising up from the provinces, a handsome man pastes the city with the blue-eyed faces of virginal girls, to show the world what is dark and foreign, dilutes. He wishes to hold the borders fast, districts and gene pools simplified to a pale reflexiveness. Late snow whitens the hair of the students, turns to slush at their booted feet.

Shame is repetitive. Shame reinvents its shades and tenor. A year ago we walked those same streets, before history bared its worm-eaten body to the air.

The Triangle Song

Two wanted to embrace a third

moved forward Stood on beach and

tipped back a head

exposed throat, made luck, turn of arm

a charm worn at neck Brought

hand to small of back let

willowy wrist go slack

Fear stood up on thin legs at the water's edge

Three walked past the snow-tipped hedge Three

mounted the gray wooden stairs

In triangles they moved about the bed

blue veins moved their red cargo south

a mouth became a cave, became a door

garments cast to floor, fabric in a crumple

It was not difficult

It was not far

the tear or cramp or turn of tissue

Enter the small form, enter the hardened muscle

fuck away the small doll

buckled in the heart's hasp

What two can do, three can do better

Feel in your head what you cut from its tether

It's Your Turn to Do the Milking, Father Said

I spent a summer dancing on a bar. It was a summer of little daylight and I was mostly imaginary. Nights I sold my calves to strangers. They looked up at my white shorts and I blinked back, distant as a wren. Sometimes I smiled for their money. Sometimes I cared. In the back room, I counted the warm bills they tucked in my waistband, damp with small effort. *I was infinitely expensive.* My heart and head followed white lines to South America where jungle birds bloomed into shrieking hats. They beat inside my chest's bone cage, called so much into possibility—bar and boot and stray foreign hand.

As a boy, I was sent to bring in the goats. They were scattered in the hills, bleating, wet eyes narrowed, bells hollowing, udders dripping sweet blue. I called and they would not come. They had seen the serpent coiled in the loafing shed, his poison mouth sprung with needles. While it struck at my shins, I chopped it into pieces with a hoe, ground its vile head in the dust with my boot. I hung the mess in a sack from a post where it twisted until sundown. I made a hatband with its skin.

I am not as I would appear, you see. There is so much you never thought me capable of. The poor goats. I brought them in and milked them, they were so un-comfortable.

Ice Queen

Place your hands together in an attitude of supplication.
Bring to me your notion of hopefulness.

In my small kingdom, the light is leaning to the colder latitudes.
The populace readies for its season of deprivation

with deep concern. Horses that once
nosed the green edges of the glacier are back

in the snow pastures where they will paw
with need deeper than hunger

though less efficient. Overhead wind moves
that is not a wind. Souls fog the harbor

with their faces of distance, cats return to the barn eaves
to lick the insides of an egg sucked dry last summer.

Your absence has taught me how the senses
might be heightened—knife-sharp

angel-heavy. Like wings, they will lift me
to my winter quarters, where a cold cup of coffee

waits, an offering to the governing powers
of abandonment. Believe me

when I say it was not always like this.
Once I was more than this lean-to in the memory.

Look at me, little body.
Look at me with a heart that is drum-empty.

Invention

Ghost, I have searched theaters of the flesh
for your imagined face, found you

among the boy whores working the carpeted hallways
of the cinema, or at the beach in late summer

your tanned thighs slipping from a sarong, urging me to compare you
to the heraldic figures.

My sweet invented one, I have loved you
more cleanly and with greater cruelty

than any actual suitor, to whom
I offered questions,

fed breakfast, or drove home.
I wander the empty house (memory).

You appear to me stock-still
in the snow-covered corn, guarding

what I have inflicted upon you—you.
I beg your forgiveness. I who invented you

brought you here to illustrate
my own sense of having once been shattered,

then destroyed you to show the world
I intended to be whole.

Grand Isle

At Grand Isle grass waves in a hot wind
At Grand Isle the pelicans sew up the horizon

The French wash fish blood from their boats
The French wash the dirt from their Mary shrines

At the corner a pale girl sells sweet ice in paper
Oh my sweet wind-bitten tongue

Men throw their nets to the brine
the rope edge bit in their teeth

while boats dip down their rusting wings

A man walks up the shell path, shirt open
ascends the stairs like a hero

Whose voice calls? Whom does he hold hot
in the chest's shuttered room?

From the deck, his skin like gold paper
What he wants is a shape the mouth makes

—the light which, showing the way, forbids it
—to wander for a spell in abysses

Letter from Bayou LaFourche

We clean out Uncle's house, take the copper pots, the Grecian bust and china Mary, her hollow center stuffed with the ring and rosary—reliquary. Uncle is leashed to this oxygen tank, diminishing. We leave the mysterious electric probe, the flaking books of recipes. Back at his rented room, he speaks in Southern innuendo. An enormous neighbor blusters across the parking lot. She has come to show us photographs of her boy who is beautiful and dangerous in New York City. Uncle sends us to buy Blue Bunny bread.

In Belle Rose, Miss Rosa Mae tells the table, *Every trashy thing on the Bayou is a friend of Henry Boudreaux.* She says, *Swamp? The whole goddamn state of Louisiana ain't nothin' but a swamp.* She says, *Cher, fix me some peanut butter and syrup. I need a little collation.* She says, *Ples Misere!* She says, *I think your car must be the tackiest thing.*

Cane fields flash past the windows of the car. Our cigarettes burn like insect eyes. At Pierre Part, fighting cocks test their leashes and comb the air with shrieking. Catahoula hog dogs pace in stilted kennels, nerves thinning them to arrow points.

We set about peeling shrimp. Spanish moss spills from the trees, pale hair. Miss Rosa Mae wipes her brow with the back of her wrist. *You know, Cher, there was a time when we did not have to do all this*

Belle Rose Fragment

Tell me the story about alligator hunting.

The one when your father took you.
The one when he was scared.

> *The water was high. I remember that.*
> *And the snakes were nesting, anywhere on high ground.*
> *There were mounds of them, twined together.*
> *It was cold and they were slow, but there were hundreds.*
> *He put me up on his shoulders.*
> *He told me to be very still.*

Then what happened?

> *I don't remember.*

The Visit

I know you're not listening
by the high fidelity of this echo—
a blizzard rung from a wet finger on crystal—

that cold. You keep coming to me
in those ridiculous sandals
I assume have some meaning

in what's left of the wilderness.
Coat of smoke, burdened traveler,
how have you managed to slip down my hallway

to sit, once more, at the edge of my bed,
your hand holding out the dusty chrysanthemums
shot through with a year's iron-scented wind?

Letter to E.

You do not know the cold the way I have known it—imperious, the driest variety. Breath becomes a spindle wound with interior heat.

With your sandals and bare arms, California chills you. In clouds of late-morning weather, you move about that sensible house, snuffing lamps one by one. As a boy soprano you hit the highest notes without vibrato, capturing collapsing centuries as the music grew.

It is true that we are savaged by decay, but what of it? Sun spoils us. Smoke will come back in spider form. And sex can spread the cruelest things, from the sweet crush of flesh in the dark, when all you want is to be inside another. Care is a virtue, but worry is a web. Books are full of the quick demise of better men than you and I, braver ones, and truer too.

In bitter weather I trust the mind. I find it better than sheepfold or stable, better than twin blades traversing the ice. Even the river froze though underneath the current still pushed, the fish slowed and done with feeding, waiting with a patience wired to their vertebrae. Cold thinned them, but they survived.

Poem Beginning with a Line by Cavafy

Brain, work now as well as you can.

Bring to me that image of his face—the one who has just left me.

Through the window last night, the traffic light

shifted red to green. On the stereo, a recording

of great complexity, through which one heard

a desert dove's small call bound

in a fine machine. Worlds have been crossed

to bring him to me. Sands covered Persia,

fourteen hills trembled in a morning quake

while an Arizona of lost hours burst in a ring of fire.

Soprano Authority

The mist persisted and the fog persisted.
The magnolia held the globes of flowers in its hands,
and the mass with its unavoidable conclusion

played on the stereo—*O Lamb of God,*
with tender steps I tread—
with its progressions—B flat, A flat minor—Rome

did burn again, did burn again.
The two lay on the floor and the fire burned
behind its grate, while the mist thickened the night,

the streetlights held their yellow globes,
and the two listened to the recorded voice
of one of the men, his voice a boy's pure soprano,

notes he will never reach again.
The two listened to the mass, with its inevitable conclusion—
the wood brace hung with the body of a man,

a sorrow so large it could contain the whole world,
the voice on the stereo a voice without ache,
without tremor, gone now,

except for this recording,
which they rewind and listen to again,
one man hearing with quickening intent,

the other listening to what he has lost—
the bell and burn and soft treading steps—
a boy's voice buried in the throat of a man.

Split Infinitives

There was an outdoor market where we shopped. Turkish women jostled us. Men beckoned from their stalls of fruit. There was a plan if we were to be separated. There was a place to meet.

A young woman leans out of her window into the courtyard, trying to dial a telephone. A bomb has fallen in a suburb of Sofia, though it did not detonate. A satellite hovers above Europe, intent on catching these female notes of concern. Americans feel their way along channels of sky, to the Balkans, strapped into fighter jets, cargoes of fuel and of fire. The safety of a continent is currently hinged.

Below the cathedral, the catacombs. Without their flesh the bones become more holy. I join the curious on their tour. Our breath assists the decay. Skulls stacked in rows like empty jars, their eyeholes a constancy. Outside again, I light a cigarette to measure the time, feel reduction.

Loss resets the needle of its soundtrack. You, the gift offered, the gift refused.

Seen

In your field of vision, there is a place where no image is fixed,

where injury carved its cave of nothing,

gathered blackness around a splinter's wooden slip.

One eye, you say, scans the world.

The other examines the self's invisible wanting.

In that equation, I believe myself to be

the point connecting one destination to another,

somewhere you paused to draw lines to the next warm station.

I emit no light, no heat

but gather, in cupped hands, what fell to the ground

when limbs were shaken by your grasping wind.

The Room

What I offered you

was more than words on paper.

Now it is as if I viewed a night sky

and saw no planet upon which

we could pin our earnest conversation.

Inside me, there is a room no one will come to.

I have shuttered its five grave windows,

swept clean its smooth, reflective floor

and the key is somewhere I don't remember.

An Argument

The city glitters in its crown of hills—

a tiny Rome crushed onto this unlikely continent,

houses jammed into blond sockets,

vines spinning tendrils up fences and over roofs.

I would possess you, if I could, but you evade me.

You are caught in your own head of curls.

What you offer me must suffice, I tell myself

though take this as my complaint:

my own head already contains you, whether or not

you will ever stroke the hair back from my face.

The Buck

I shot the buck and he crumpled,

folded like a ladder into the snow.

He had bounded along a worn path,

jumped a fallen log and paused,

turning his flank toward me

and I saw his nostrils flare

through the ocular concentration

of a rifle's scope. I placed the red bead

of the sight on the fur covering the spot

above the twin bellows of his lungs,

and squeezed the trigger to release the shot.

There was a pause after the rifle's report

during which my heart and the buck's surged,

though only mine would propel me into a future,

in which I bore a knife and numerous pockets,

carried a lanyard that I would lash

to the buck's antler rack and drag him

down a logging road to the stubbled field.

    Why did you shoot the deer?

Because we were hunting.

    Did you enjoy it? The hunting?

I'm not sure. I think I did.

    I mean, did you enjoy it when you killed?

Yes.

    What was enjoyable?

I was powerful. I could put an end to something independent.

    That's an enjoyable thing?

No. Something changes, just before the fatal moment.

    Yes? What changed?

I saw the future.

Tamed

That summer I broke a gelding. For a year I taught him to arc toward the handle of my whip, tensing. He grew, though I remained small, a boy made thin by the rigors of an imaginary life. When I strapped the saddle on, his eyes rolled like romantic clouds. He snorted as his future became smaller. Later, I sat upon his back, which had only borne the weight of insects. He braced himself and walked stiffly in a circle. He hated me instantly.

When the milkweeds blew their pods in the pasture, he knew to stand while I slipped my boot into the metal D. He knew the taste of metal though I warmed the snaffle in my fist before he took it in. My short spurs urged him into five gaits.

I had a suit made—vest, jacket and jodhpurs, all in officious blue. I bought a bridle and girth to match. He was sufficiently tamed.

I was thrown several times. Each time I rose up from the dust to catch him by the reins. It wasn't discouraging. I knew I deserved it.

On Omens

Today, the sky is boiling.

Hear me out. It is heated from something down here.

The clouds are fulminating and branching in skeins of wire.

They are pricked by needles of heat rising off a paved world.

It is June, and already the garden is a failure.

Plants spindle under the wan light,

stalks blight and waver down to the hairs of their roots.

I would try to tell you how it feels to be your captive,

but there's something hatching in my throat,

clouding my words, eating my cells.

We think we are safe.

On my birthday, when ice coated the telephone wires

and juncos pecked millet from the snow,

in the light from the neighbor's porch,

I saw two coyotes cross the yard in dark silhouette.

They sniffed the ground for cats

then disappeared beyond the hedge.

I tried to see them as an omen.

They weren't an omen.

They were too hungry for that.

Town, Gone

He touched the back of his neck,
forked his fingers through red hair,
and the trees breathed their dioxide in the street,

and the gulls waved their cuts,
in the air, and I asked if this
was what he meant, the static,

and he nodded, and I looked down
at my hands touching
the only skin they'll own,

and he moved to touch my hair,
hair grown pale in the winter, silver
like the iced trees in half-light

and I asked what could break
or trouble the form
our lives had taken and he said

he didn't know, but I knew
that this was how it would be
and the town in my head

where my inventions moved
in their elaborate machines, their dramas
and re-enactments, their closing doors

and sweeping, their papers
rifled through and tested for accuracy,
that town began to empty

until the room was full of that population,
and they were of me and I
was of them, and they

broke into pieces, a windshield
gone through, and left
in fragments through the window

I cracked to let out the smoke,
left me looking down at my hands
and I knew I'd never hear them again

and that they were the smoke
and—town gone, vast catastrophe—
I was what they left behind in the fire.

The Meeting

Did I say it was a walk in the forest?

Well then. Very well.

There were trails in the forest that were sand-covered.

That is to say, domesticated.

There were signs of footprints, but no people.

Through the trees, a distant beach shook itself with tidal changes.

The waves heaved, a watery lung.

What was it like to touch him?

It is difficult to say. I will try to remember.

I recall only the weight of an arm,

trees crossing out the sun

and a path leading out into the open.

Notes

"Device for Burning Bees and Sugar" borrows its title from a sculpture of the same name by artist Nayland Blake.

"I Too Am an Animal of Great Beauty" takes its title from an unpublished journal entry by Taylor Meade.

The italicized line in "It's Your Turn to Do the Milking, Father Said" paraphrases a line from Sylvia Plath's poem "Fever 103°"

The final italicized lines of "Grand Isle" are taken from Kate Chopin's novel *The Awakening.*

"Poem Beginning with a Line by Cavafy" quotes his poem "A Young Poet in His Twenty-Fourth Year," which is translated by Edmund Keeley and Philip Sherrard.

Acknowledgments

Grateful acknowledgment is made to the editors of the following publications in which some of these poems have appeared:

Boston Review: "Town," "Gone"
Chelsea: "Error," "Vulpecular Dream #1"
Chicago Review: "Obedience Attempts," "The Kept One"
Columbia: "Tamed"
Denver Quarterly: "Breakable," "The Imperial Life of Insects," "I Too Am an Animal of Great Beauty"
Electronic Poetry Review: "Dream of Archeology," "Landscape Dream #7"
Fence: "The Visit," "Voluntary Servitude"
Green Mountains Review: "Belle Rose Fragment," "Grand Isle," "On Omens," "Split Infinitives," "The Buck"
Jubilat: "Postcards from the Vienna Woods"
Lumina: "Ice Queen"
Nerve.com: "The Triangle Song"
New England Review: "The Meeting," "Poem Beginning with a Line by Cavafy," "Lamb," "Dream: Intruder," "Water Snake"
The Paris Review: "Tack," "White"
Ploughshares: "Seen"
Pool: "Invention"
Post Road: "It's Your Turn to Do the Milking, Father Said," "Device for Burning Bees and Sugar"
Slate: "Amaryllis"
The Southeast Review: "Letter from Bayou LaFourche," "Letter to E.," "Letter to J."
Western Humanities Review: "An Argument"
The Yale Review: "Soprano Authority"

"Tack" was also published as a limited edition broadside by the Center for Book Arts, New York, NY.

"Amaryllis" also appeared in *Vespers: Contemporary American Poems of Religion and Spirituality;* University of Iowa Press, 2003.

I would like to thank the Fine Arts Work Center in Provincetown, the Wallace Stegner Fellowship Program at Stanford University, and the Massachusetts Cultural Council for fellowships that made possible the completion of this book.

I owe a debt of gratitude to Mary Jo Bang, Erin Belieu, Mary Jane Dean, Sarah Messer, Carmen Gimenez-Roselló, Marc Schachter, Katharine Whitcomb, and Monica Youn.

MARK WUNDERLICH is the author of three books of poetry: *The Earth Avails,* *Voluntary Servitude,* and *The Anchorage,* which received the 1999 Lambda Literary Award. He has been the recipient of two fellowships from the Fine Arts Work Center in Provincetown, the Wallace Stegner Fellowship from Stanford University, and the Amy Lowell Traveling Fellowship. He lives in New York's Hudson River Valley and is Professor of Literature at Bennington College in Vermont.

Book design by Wendy Holdman.
Composition by BookMobile Design and
Publisher Services, Minneapolis, Minnesota.
Manufactured by BookMobile on acid-free
30 percent postconsumer wastepaper.